MY

RECIPES

MEASURING CONVERSIONS

CUP		Tbsp		Tsp
1/4	=	4	=	12
1/3	=	5	=	16
1/2	=	8	=	24
2/3	=	11	=	32
3/4	=	12	=	36
1	=	16	=	48

SLOW COOKER TEMP

LOW	HIGH
7 hours	3 hours
8 hours	4 hours
9 hours	5 hours
10 hours	6 hours
11 hours	7 hours
12 hours	8 hours

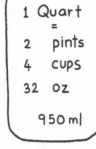

1 Quart
=
2 pints
4 cups
32 oz

950 ml

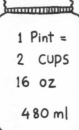

1 Pint =
2 cups
16 oz

480 ml

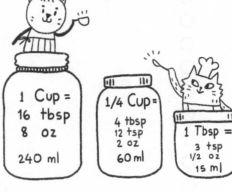

1 Cup =
16 tbsp
8 oz

240 ml

1/4 Cup=
4 tbsp
12 tsp
2 oz
60 ml

1 Tbsp =
3 tsp
1/2 oz
15 ml

RECIPE

RECIPE

PAGE

RECIPE:

FROM THE
KITCHEN OF _____

SERVES _____

INGREDIENTS

_____
_____
_____
_____
_____
_____
_____
_____
_____
_____
_____
_____

INSTRUCTIONS

_____
_____
_____
_____
_____
_____
_____
_____
_____
_____
_____
_____
_____
_____
_____
_____
_____
_____
_____
_____

NOTES

_____

_____

_____

_____

_____

○ EXCELLENT

○ GOOD

○ FAIR

○ NEVER AGAIN

RECILPE:

FROM THE
KITCHEN OF _____

SERVES _____

PREP TIME ⬭

COOK TIME ⬭

COOLING TIME ⬭

TOTAL TIME ⬭

MINUTES

INGREDIENTS

INSTRUCTIONS

8

NOTES

_____

_____

_____

_____

_____

EXCELLENT

GOOD

FAIR

NEVER AGAIN

RECIPE:

FROM THE
KITCHEN OF _____

SERVES _____

PREP TIME ⬭

COOK TIME ⬭

COOLING TIME ⬭

TOTAL TIME ⬭

MINUTES

INGREDIENTS

_____
_____
_____
_____
_____
_____
_____
_____
_____
_____
_____
_____
_____
_____

INSTRUCTIONS

_____
_____
_____
_____
_____
_____
_____
_____
_____
_____
_____
_____
_____
_____
_____
_____
_____
_____
_____
_____

NOTES

_____

_____

_____

_____

_____

○ ⭐☆ EXCELLENT

○ ⭐☆ GOOD

○ FAIR

○ NEVER AGAIN

PREP TIME ⬭ MINUTES

COOK TIME ⬭

COOLING TIME ⬭

TOTAL TIME ⬭

MY ♥ RECIPE

SERVES

INGREDIENTS

_____

_____

_____

_____

_____

_____

_____

_____

_____

_____

_____

_____

NOTES

INSTRUCTIONS

_____

_____

_____

_____

_____

_____

_____

_____

_____

_____

_____

_____

_____

_____

_____

_____

_____

_____

_____

NOTES

_____

_____

_____

_____

_____

○ EXCELLENT

○ GOOD

○ FAIR

○ NEVER AGAIN

PREP TIME   MINUTES

COOK TIME

COOLING TIME

TOTAL TIME

RECIPE

FROM THE
KITCHEN OF _____

SERVES _____

INGREDIENTS

INSTRUCTIONS

NOTES

14

NOTES

_____
_____
_____
_____
_____
_____

○ EXCELLENT

○ GOOD

○ FAIR

○ NEVER AGAIN

RECIPE:

FROM THE
KITCHEN OF _____

SERVES _____

PREP TIME

COOK TIME

COOLING TIME

TOTAL TIME

MINUTES

INGREDIENTS

INSTRUCTIONS

NOTES

_____

_____

_____

_____

_____

○ EXCELLENT

○ GOOD

○ FAIR

○ NEVER AGAIN

17

RECIPE:

FROM THE
KITCHEN OF _____

SERVES _____

PREP TIME ⬭

COOK TIME ⬭

COOLING TIME ⬭

TOTAL TIME ⬭

MINUTES

INGREDIENTS

_____
_____
_____
_____
_____
_____
_____
_____
_____
_____
_____
_____
_____
_____

INSTRUCTIONS

_____
_____
_____
_____
_____
_____
_____
_____
_____
_____
_____
_____
_____
_____
_____
_____
_____
_____

NOTES

_____

_____

_____

_____

_____

○ *☆ EXCELLENT

○ *☆ GOOD

○ FAIR

○ NEVER AGAIN

RECICE:

FROM THE
KITCHEN OF _____

SERVES _____

PREP TIME ◯ MINUTES
COOK TIME ◯
COOLING TIME ◯
TOTAL TIME ◯

INGREDIENTS

_____
_____
_____
_____
_____
_____
_____
_____
_____
_____
_____
_____
_____
_____
_____

INSTRUCTIONS

_____
_____
_____
_____
_____
_____
_____
_____
_____
_____
_____
_____
_____
_____
_____
_____
_____
_____
_____
_____

NOTES

_____

_____

_____

_____

_____

EXCELLENT

GOOD

FAIR

NEVER
AGAIN

PREP TIME

COOK TIME

COOLING TIME

TOTAL TIME

MINUTES

MY ♥ RECIPE

SERVES

INGREDIENTS

INSTRUCTIONS

NOTES

NOTES

_____

_____

_____

_____

_____

○ EXCELLENT

○ GOOD

○ FAIR

○ NEVER AGAIN

PREP TIME ⬭ MINUTES

COOK TIME ⬭

COOLING TIME ⬭

TOTAL TIME ⬭

RECIPE

FROM THE
KITCHEN OF _____

SERVES _____

INGREDIENTS

_____
_____
_____
_____
_____
_____
_____
_____
_____
_____
_____
_____

NOTES

INSTRUCTIONS

_____
_____
_____
_____
_____
_____
_____
_____
_____
_____
_____
_____
_____
_____
_____
_____
_____
_____
_____
_____
_____
_____

NOTES

_____

_____

_____

_____

_____

_____

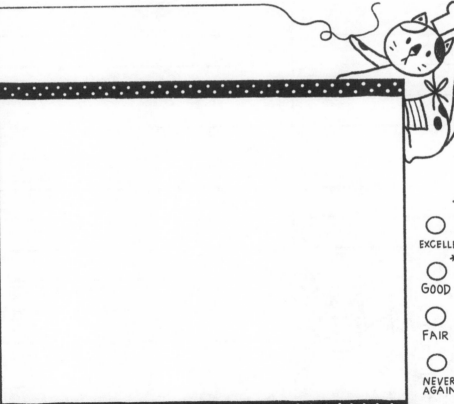

EXCELLENT

GOOD

FAIR

NEVER
AGAIN

RECIPE:

FROM THE
KITCHEN OF _____

SERVES _____

PREP TIME ◯
COOK TIME ◯
COOLING TIME ◯
TOTAL TIME ◯

MINUTES

INGREDIENTS

INSTRUCTIONS

NOTES

_____

_____

_____

_____

_____

○ EXCELLENT

○ GOOD

○ FAIR

○ NEVER AGAIN

RECIPE:

FROM THE
KITCHEN OF _____

SERVES _____

PREP TIME ⬭
COOK TIME ⬭
COOLING TIME ⬭
TOTAL TIME ⬭

MINUTES

INGREDIENTS

_____
_____
_____
_____
_____
_____
_____
_____
_____
_____
_____

INSTRUCTIONS

_____
_____
_____
_____
_____
_____
_____
_____
_____
_____
_____
_____
_____
_____
_____

NOTES

_____

_____

_____

_____

_____

EXCELLENT

GOOD

FAIR

NEVER AGAIN

RECIPE:

FROM THE
KITCHEN OF _____

SERVES _____

PREP TIME ⬭ MINUTES

COOK TIME ⬭

COOLING TIME ⬭

TOTAL TIME ⬭

INGREDIENTS

_____
_____
_____
_____
_____
_____
_____
_____
_____
_____
_____
_____
_____
_____
_____

INSTRUCTIONS

_____
_____
_____
_____
_____
_____
_____
_____
_____
_____
_____
_____
_____
_____
_____
_____
_____
_____
_____
_____

NOTES

EXCELLENT

GOOD

FAIR

NEVER
AGAIN

PREP TIME $\quad$ ◯ MINUTES

COOK TIME $\quad$ ◯

COOLING TIME $\quad$ ◯

TOTAL TIME $\quad$ ◯

MY ♥ RECIPE

SERVES

INGREDIENTS

_____
_____
_____
_____
_____
_____
_____
_____
_____
_____
_____
_____
_____

NOTES

INSTRUCTIONS

_____
_____
_____
_____
_____
_____
_____
_____
_____
_____
_____
_____
_____
_____
_____
_____
_____
_____
_____
_____
_____
_____

NOTES

EXCELLENT

GOOD

FAIR

NEVER AGAIN

PREP TIME ⬭ MINUTES

COOK TIME ⬭

COOLING TIME ⬭

TOTAL TIME ⬭

🍴 RECIPE 🍴

FROM THE
KITCHEN OF _____

SERVES _____

INGREDIENTS

_____
_____
_____
_____
_____
_____
_____
_____
_____
_____
_____
_____
_____

NOTES

INSTRUCTIONS

_____
_____
_____
_____
_____
_____
_____
_____
_____
_____
_____
_____
_____
_____
_____
_____
_____
_____
_____
_____
_____
_____
_____

NOTES

_____

_____

_____

_____

_____

_____

○ ✦✧ EXCELLENT

○ ✦✧ GOOD

○ FAIR

○ NEVER AGAIN

RECIPE:

PREP TIME
COOK TIME
COOLING TIME
TOTAL TIME

MINUTES

FROM THE
KITCHEN OF _____

SERVES _____

INGREDIENTS

_____
_____
_____
_____
_____
_____
_____
_____
_____
_____
_____
_____
_____
_____
_____
_____

INSTRUCTIONS

_____
_____
_____
_____
_____
_____
_____
_____
_____
_____
_____
_____
_____
_____
_____
_____
_____
_____
_____

NOTES

_____
_____
_____
_____
_____

○ EXCELLENT

○ GOOD

○ FAIR

○ NEVER AGAIN

RECIPE:

FROM THE
KITCHEN OF _____

SERVES _____

PREP TIME ⬭

COOK TIME ⬭

COOLING TIME ⬭

TOTAL TIME ⬭

MINUTES

INGREDIENTS

_____
_____
_____
_____
_____
_____
_____
_____
_____
_____
_____
_____
_____
_____

INSTRUCTIONS

_____
_____
_____
_____
_____
_____
_____
_____
_____
_____
_____
_____
_____
_____
_____
_____
_____
_____
_____
_____
_____

NOTES

_____

_____

_____

_____

_____

EXCELLENT

GOOD

FAIR

NEVER
AGAIN

RECITE:

FROM THE
KITCHEN OF _____

SERVES _____

INGREDIENTS

_____
_____
_____
_____
_____
_____
_____
_____
_____
_____
_____
_____
_____
_____
_____

INSTRUCTIONS

_____
_____
_____
_____
_____
_____
_____
_____
_____
_____
_____
_____
_____
_____
_____
_____
_____
_____
_____
_____

40

NOTES

_____

_____

_____

_____

_____

EXCELLENT

GOOD

FAIR

NEVER
AGAIN

41

PREP TIME ⬭ MINUTES

COOK TIME ⬭

COOLING TIME ⬭

TOTAL TIME ⬭

MY ♥ RECIPE

SERVES

INGREDIENTS

INSTRUCTIONS

NOTES

NOTES

_____

_____

_____

_____

_____

EXCELLENT

GOOD

FAIR

NEVER
AGAIN

PREP TIME

COOK TIME

COOLING TIME

TOTAL TIME

MINUTES

RECIPE

FROM THE
KITCHEN OF _____

SERVES _____

INGREDIENTS

_____
_____
_____
_____
_____
_____
_____
_____
_____
_____
_____
_____
_____

NOTES

INSTRUCTIONS

_____
_____
_____
_____
_____
_____
_____
_____
_____
_____
_____
_____
_____
_____
_____
_____
_____
_____
_____
_____
_____

NOTES

_____

_____

_____

_____

_____

_____

○ EXCELLENT

○ GOOD

○ FAIR

○ NEVER AGAIN

45

RECIPE:

PREP TIME ◯

COOK TIME ◯

COOLING TIME ◯

TOTAL TIME ◯

MINUTES

FROM THE
KITCHEN OF _____

SERVES _____

INGREDIENTS

_____
_____
_____
_____
_____
_____
_____
_____
_____
_____
_____
_____
_____

INSTRUCTIONS

_____
_____
_____
_____
_____
_____
_____
_____
_____
_____
_____
_____
_____
_____
_____
_____
_____
_____
_____

NOTES

_____

_____

_____

_____

_____

○ EXCELLENT

○ GOOD

○ FAIR

○ NEVER AGAIN

RECITE:

FROM THE
KITCHEN OF _____

SERVES _____

PREP TIME ◯ MINUTES

COOK TIME ◯

COOLING TIME ◯

TOTAL TIME ◯

INGREDIENTS

_____
_____
_____
_____
_____
_____
_____
_____
_____
_____
_____
_____
_____
_____

INSTRUCTIONS

_____
_____
_____
_____
_____
_____
_____
_____
_____
_____
_____
_____
_____
_____
_____
_____
_____
_____
_____
_____
_____
_____

 NOTES

_____

_____

_____

_____

_____

○ EXCELLENT

○ GOOD

○ FAIR

○ NEVER AGAIN

RECIPE:

FROM THE
KITCHEN OF _____

SERVES _____

PREP TIME ◯
COOK TIME ◯
COOLING TIME ◯
TOTAL TIME ◯

MINUTES

INGREDIENTS

INSTRUCTIONS

NOTES

_____

_____

_____

_____

_____

EXCELLENT

GOOD

FAIR

NEVER AGAIN

PREP TIME ⬭ MINUTES

COOK TIME ⬭

COOLING TIME ⬭

TOTAL TIME ⬭

MY ♥ RECIPE

SERVES

INGREDIENTS 🌿

_____
_____
_____
_____
_____
_____
_____
_____
_____
_____
_____
_____
_____
_____
_____
_____

🍲 NOTES

INSTRUCTIONS

_____
_____
_____
_____
_____
_____
_____
_____
_____
_____
_____
_____
_____
_____
_____
_____
_____
_____
_____
_____
_____
_____

NOTES

_____

_____

_____

_____

_____

EXCELLENT

GOOD

FAIR

NEVER
AGAIN

PREP TIME ◯ MINUTES

COOK TIME ◯

COOLING TIME ◯

TOTAL TIME ◯

RECIPE

FROM THE
KITCHEN OF _____

SERVES _____

INGREDIENTS

_____
_____
_____
_____
_____
_____
_____
_____
_____
_____
_____
_____
_____

NOTES

INSTRUCTIONS

_____
_____
_____
_____
_____
_____
_____
_____
_____
_____
_____
_____
_____
_____
_____
_____
_____
_____
_____
_____
_____
_____
_____

NOTES

_____

_____

_____

_____

_____

EXCELLENT

GOOD

FAIR

NEVER
AGAIN

RECIPE:

FROM THE
KITCHEN OF _____

SERVES _____

PREP TIME ⬭
COOK TIME ⬭
COOLING TIME ⬭
TOTAL TIME ⬭

MINUTES

INGREDIENTS

INSTRUCTIONS

NOTES

_____

_____

_____

_____

_____

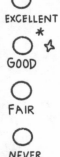

○ EXCELLENT

○ GOOD

○ FAIR

○ NEVER AGAIN

RECIPE:

PREP TIME ◯ MINUTES

COOK TIME ◯

COOLING TIME ◯

TOTAL TIME ◯

FROM THE
KITCHEN OF _____

SERVES _____

INGREDIENTS

_____
_____
_____
_____
_____
_____
_____
_____
_____
_____
_____
_____
_____
_____
_____
_____

INSTRUCTIONS

_____
_____
_____
_____
_____
_____
_____
_____
_____
_____
_____
_____
_____
_____
_____
_____
_____
_____
_____
_____
_____
_____

NOTES

_____

_____

_____

_____

_____

○ EXCELLENT

○ GOOD

○ FAIR

○ NEVER AGAIN

RECIPE:

FROM THE
KITCHEN OF _____

SERVES _____

PREP TIME ◯

COOK TIME ◯

COOLING TIME ◯

TOTAL TIME ◯

MINUTES

INGREDIENTS

_____
_____
_____
_____
_____
_____
_____
_____
_____
_____
_____
_____

INSTRUCTIONS

_____
_____
_____
_____
_____
_____
_____
_____
_____
_____
_____
_____
_____
_____
_____
_____
_____
_____

NOTES

_____

_____

_____

_____

_____

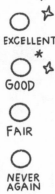

○ EXCELLENT

○ GOOD

○ FAIR

○ NEVER AGAIN

61

PREP TIME (MINUTES)

COOK TIME ( )

COOLING TIME ( )

TOTAL TIME ( )

MY ♥ RECIPE

SERVES

INGREDIENTS

INSTRUCTIONS

NOTES

62

NOTES

_____

_____

_____

_____

_____

○ EXCELLENT

○ GOOD

○ FAIR

○ NEVER AGAIN

PREP TIME   ◯ MINUTES

COOK TIME   ◯

COOLING TIME ◯

TOTAL TIME ◯

🍴 RECIPE 🍴

FROM THE
KITCHEN OF _____

SERVES _____

INGREDIENTS

INSTRUCTIONS

NOTES

NOTES

_____

_____

_____

_____

_____

_____

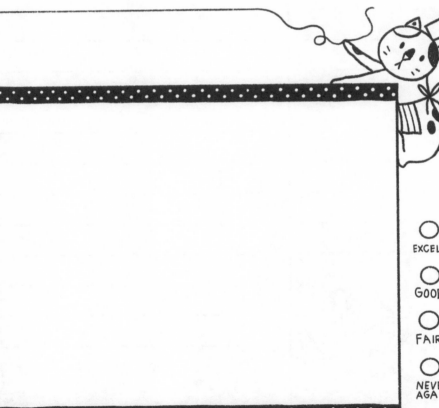

EXCELLENT

GOOD

FAIR

NEVER
AGAIN

RECIPE:

FROM THE
KITCHEN OF _____

SERVES _____

PREP TIME

COOK TIME

COOLING TIME

TOTAL TIME

MINUTES

INGREDIENTS

_____
_____
_____
_____
_____
_____
_____
_____
_____
_____
_____
_____
_____
_____

INSTRUCTIONS

_____
_____
_____
_____
_____
_____
_____
_____
_____
_____
_____
_____
_____
_____
_____
_____
_____
_____
_____

NOTES

_____

_____

_____

_____

_____

○ EXCELLENT

○ GOOD

○ FAIR

○ NEVER AGAIN

RECIPE:

FROM THE
KITCHEN OF _____

SERVES _____

PREP TIME ◯

COOK TIME ◯

COOLING TIME ◯

TOTAL TIME ◯

MINUTES

INGREDIENTS

INSTRUCTIONS

NOTES

_____

_____

_____

_____

_____

EXCELLENT

GOOD

FAIR

NEVER
AGAIN

69

RECIPE:

FROM THE
KITCHEN OF _____

SERVES _____

PREP TIME ⬭
COOK TIME ⬭
COOLING TIME ⬭
TOTAL TIME ⬭

MINUTES

INGREDIENTS

INSTRUCTIONS

NOTES

_____

_____

_____

_____

_____

EXCELLENT

GOOD

FAIR

NEVER
AGAIN

PREP TIME ⬭ MINUTES

COOK TIME ⬭

COOLING TIME ⬭

TOTAL TIME ⬭

MY ♥ RECIPE

SERVES

INGREDIENTS

INSTRUCTIONS

NOTES

NOTES

_____

_____

_____

_____

_____

EXCELLENT

GOOD

FAIR

NEVER
AGAIN

PREP TIME (MINUTES)

COOK TIME ( )

COOLING TIME ( )

TOTAL TIME ( )

RECIPE

FROM THE
KITCHEN OF _____

SERVES _____

INGREDIENTS

_____
_____
_____
_____
_____
_____
_____
_____
_____
_____
_____
_____

NOTES

INSTRUCTIONS

_____
_____
_____
_____
_____
_____
_____
_____
_____
_____
_____
_____
_____
_____
_____
_____
_____
_____
_____
_____
_____
_____

NOTES

○ EXCELLENT

○ GOOD

○ FAIR

○ NEVER
   AGAIN

RECIPE:

FROM THE
KITCHEN OF _____

SERVES _____

PREP TIME ◯
COOK TIME ◯
COOLING TIME ◯
TOTAL TIME ◯

MINUTES

INGREDIENTS

INSTRUCTIONS

NOTES

_____

_____

_____

_____

_____

○ EXCELLENT

○ GOOD

○ FAIR

○ NEVER AGAIN

RECIPE:

FROM THE
KITCHEN OF _____

SERVES _____

PREP TIME ⬭
COOK TIME ⬭
COOLING TIME ⬭
TOTAL TIME ⬭

MINUTES

INGREDIENTS

_____
_____
_____
_____
_____
_____
_____
_____
_____
_____
_____
_____
_____

INSTRUCTIONS

_____
_____
_____
_____
_____
_____
_____
_____
_____
_____
_____
_____
_____
_____
_____
_____
_____

NOTES

_____
_____
_____
_____
_____

○ EXCELLENT

○ GOOD

○ FAIR

○ NEVER AGAIN

RECIPE:

FROM THE
KITCHEN OF _____

SERVES _____

PREP TIME ⬭
COOK TIME ⬭
COOLING TIME ⬭
TOTAL TIME ⬭

MINUTES

INGREDIENTS

INSTRUCTIONS

NOTES

_____

_____

_____

_____

_____

○ EXCELLENT

○ GOOD

○ FAIR

○ NEVER AGAIN

81

PREP TIME ⬭ MINUTES

COOK TIME ⬭

COOLING TIME ⬭

TOTAL TIME ⬭

MY ♥ RECIPE

SERVES

INGREDIENTS

INSTRUCTIONS

NOTES

NOTES

_____

_____

_____

_____

_____

○ EXCELLENT

○ GOOD

○ FAIR

○ NEVER AGAIN

PREP TIME

COOK TIME

COOLING TIME

TOTAL TIME

MINUTES

RECIPE

FROM THE
KITCHEN OF _____

SERVES _____

INGREDIENTS

INSTRUCTIONS

NOTES

NOTES

EXCELLENT

GOOD

FAIR

NEVER
AGAIN

RECIPE:

PREP TIME

COOK TIME

COOLING TIME

TOTAL TIME

FROM THE
KITCHEN OF _____

SERVES _____

INGREDIENTS

INSTRUCTIONS

NOTES

_____

_____

_____

_____

_____

○
EXCELLENT

○
GOOD

○
FAIR

○
NEVER
AGAIN

RECIPE:

FROM THE
KITCHEN OF _____

SERVES _____

PREP TIME ⬭ MINUTES

COOK TIME ⬭

COOLING TIME ⬭

TOTAL TIME ⬭

INGREDIENTS

INSTRUCTIONS

NOTES

_____
_____
_____
_____
_____

○ EXCELLENT

○ GOOD

○ FAIR

○ NEVER AGAIN

RECIPE:

FROM THE
KITCHEN OF _____

SERVES _____

PREP TIME ⬭
COOK TIME ⬭
COOLING TIME ⬭
TOTAL TIME ⬭

MINUTES

INGREDIENTS

INSTRUCTIONS

NOTES

_____

_____

_____

_____

_____

EXCELLENT

GOOD

FAIR

NEVER AGAIN

PREP TIME   MINUTES

COOK TIME

COOLING TIME

TOTAL TIME

MY ♥ RECIPE

SERVES

INGREDIENTS

INSTRUCTIONS

NOTES

NOTES

_____
_____
_____
_____
_____

EXCELLENT

GOOD

FAIR

NEVER
AGAIN

PREP TIME ( ) MINUTES

COOK TIME ( )

COOLING TIME ( )

TOTAL TIME ( )

RECIPE

FROM THE
KITCHEN OF _____

SERVES _____

INGREDIENTS

_____
_____
_____
_____
_____
_____
_____
_____
_____
_____
_____
_____
_____
_____

NOTES

INSTRUCTIONS

_____
_____
_____
_____
_____
_____
_____
_____
_____
_____
_____
_____
_____
_____
_____
_____
_____
_____
_____
_____
_____
_____
_____
_____
_____
_____
_____

NOTES

_____

_____

_____

_____

_____

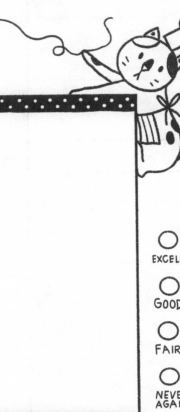

○ EXCELLENT

○ GOOD

○ FAIR

○ NEVER AGAIN

RECIPE:

PREP TIME

COOK TIME

COOLING TIME

TOTAL TIME

MINUTES

FROM THE
KITCHEN OF _____

SERVES _____

INGREDIENTS

_____
_____
_____
_____
_____
_____
_____
_____
_____
_____
_____
_____
_____
_____

INSTRUCTIONS

_____
_____
_____
_____
_____
_____
_____
_____
_____
_____
_____
_____
_____
_____
_____
_____
_____
_____
_____

 NOTES

_____

_____

_____

_____

_____

EXCELLENT

GOOD

FAIR

NEVER
AGAIN

RECIPE:

FROM THE
KITCHEN OF _____

SERVES _____

PREP TIME ◯

COOK TIME ◯

COOLING TIME ◯

TOTAL TIME ◯

MINUTES

INGREDIENTS

INSTRUCTIONS

 NOTES

_____

_____

_____

_____

_____

○ EXCELLENT

○ GOOD

○ FAIR

○ NEVER AGAIN

RECIPE:

FROM THE
KITCHEN OF _____

SERVES _____

PREP TIME ⬭
COOK TIME ⬭
COOLING TIME ⬭
TOTAL TIME ⬭

MINUTES

INGREDIENTS

INSTRUCTIONS

NOTES

_____

_____

_____

_____

_____

EXCELLENT

GOOD

FAIR

NEVER
AGAIN

PREP TIME (MINUTES)

COOK TIME ( )

COOLING TIME ( )

TOTAL TIME ( )

MY ♥ RECIPE

SERVES

INGREDIENTS

INSTRUCTIONS

NOTES

NOTES

_____

_____

_____

_____

_____

○ ⭐ EXCELLENT

○ ⭐ GOOD

○ FAIR

○ NEVER AGAIN

PREP TIME ⬭ MINUTES

COOK TIME ⬭

COOLING TIME ⬭

TOTAL TIME ⬭

🍴RECIPE🍴

FROM THE
KITCHEN OF _____

SERVES _____

INGREDIENTS

_____
_____
_____
_____
_____
_____
_____
_____
_____
_____
_____
_____
_____
_____
_____

NOTES
::::::::::::

INSTRUCTIONS

_____
_____
_____
_____
_____
_____
_____
_____
_____
_____
_____
_____
_____
_____
_____
_____
_____
_____
_____
_____
_____

NOTES

○ EXCELLENT

○ GOOD

○ FAIR

○ NEVER AGAIN

RECIPE:

FROM THE
KITCHEN OF _____

SERVES _____

PREP TIME

COOK TIME

COOLING TIME

TOTAL TIME

MINUTES

INGREDIENTS

INSTRUCTIONS

NOTES

_____
_____
_____
_____
_____

EXCELLENT

GOOD

FAIR

NEVER
AGAIN

RECIPE:

FROM THE
KITCHEN OF _____

SERVES _____

PREP TIME ⬭

COOK TIME ⬭

COOLING TIME ⬭

TOTAL TIME ⬭

MINUTES

INGREDIENTS

_____
_____
_____
_____
_____
_____
_____
_____
_____
_____
_____
_____

INSTRUCTIONS

_____
_____
_____
_____
_____
_____
_____
_____
_____
_____
_____
_____
_____
_____
_____
_____
_____
_____

NOTES

_____

_____

_____

_____

_____

○ EXCELLENT

○ GOOD

○ FAIR

○ NEVER AGAIN

RECIPE:

FROM THE
KITCHEN OF _____

SERVES _____

PREP TIME ⬭

COOK TIME ⬭

COOLING TIME ⬭

TOTAL TIME ⬭

MINUTES

INGREDIENTS

_____
_____
_____
_____
_____
_____
_____
_____
_____
_____
_____

INSTRUCTIONS

_____
_____
_____
_____
_____
_____
_____
_____
_____
_____
_____
_____
_____
_____
_____
_____

NOTES

_____

_____

_____

_____

_____

EXCELLENT

GOOD

FAIR

NEVER AGAIN

PREP TIME ⬭ MINUTES

COOK TIME ⬭

COOLING TIME ⬭

TOTAL TIME ⬭

MY ♥ RECIPE

SERVES

INGREDIENTS

INSTRUCTIONS

NOTES

NOTES

_____

_____

_____

_____

_____

EXCELLENT

GOOD

FAIR

NEVER
AGAIN

PREP TIME ⬭ MINUTES

COOK TIME ⬭

COOLING TIME ⬭

TOTAL TIME ⬭

RECIPE

FROM THE
KITCHEN OF _____

SERVES _____

INGREDIENTS

_____
_____
_____
_____
_____
_____
_____
_____
_____
_____
_____
_____
_____
_____
_____

NOTES

INSTRUCTIONS

_____
_____
_____
_____
_____
_____
_____
_____
_____
_____
_____
_____
_____
_____
_____
_____
_____
_____
_____
_____
_____
_____
_____
_____
_____

NOTES

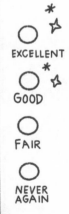

○ EXCELLENT

○ GOOD

○ FAIR

○ NEVER AGAIN

MY NEXT RECIPES

Made in United States
Troutdale, OR
12/02/2023

15235975R20076